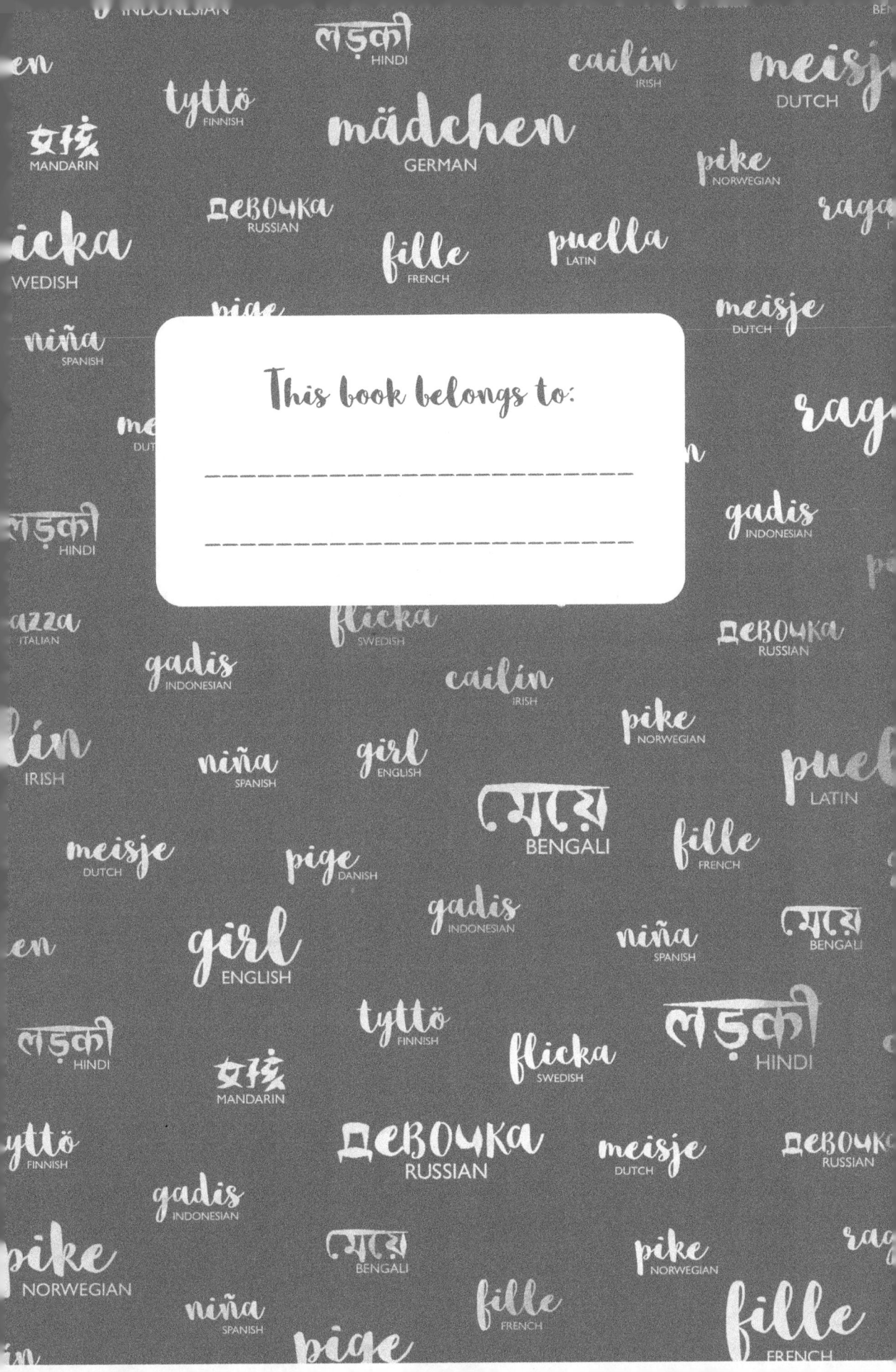

Published in 2021 by Connor Court Publishing Pty Ltd

Copyright © Wendy Francis

All rights reserved. No part of this book may be reproduced or transmitted in any form or by any means, electronic or mechanical, including photocopying, recording or by any information storage and retrieval system, without prior permission in writing from the publisher.

Connor Court Publishing Pty Ltd
PO Box 7257
Redland Bay QLD 4165
sales@connorcourt.com
www.connorcourtpublishing.com.au

Phone 0497 900 685

ISBN: 9781925826357

Front Cover Design: E.G. Turnbull
Illustrator: E.G. Turnbull
Front Cover Photo: unsplash
Picture Credits: unsplash, pexels

Printed in Australia

WHAT ARE LITTLE GIRLS MADE OF?

"speaking the truth in love"
Ephesians 4:15

WENDY FRANCIS

It's a girl!

In many different languages
these are the first words a baby girl
will hear after she is born.

In that minute,
    she has no idea what it
        means to be born a girl and
    how much promise there is in
        that one word!

But one thing she can be sure of.

She is a girl and that is awesome.

You don't get to decide if you're
born a girl or a boy –
you just are!
And you are exactly who you are
meant to be.

Girls are different to boys,
  but they are not better or worse.

They are equal, and different.

Little girls behave the same as boys in lots of ways.

Girls and boys enjoy lots of the same things.

Like walking in the sunshine,
reading a good book, or
sitting and talking with friends.

So, what makes a girl, a girl?

Girls and boys bodies are different.
Let's look at some of the science.
Human beings have been created with
twenty-three pairs of building blocks that
are called chromosomes.

These amazing structures carry information about who you are and determine everything from your height to your eye color.

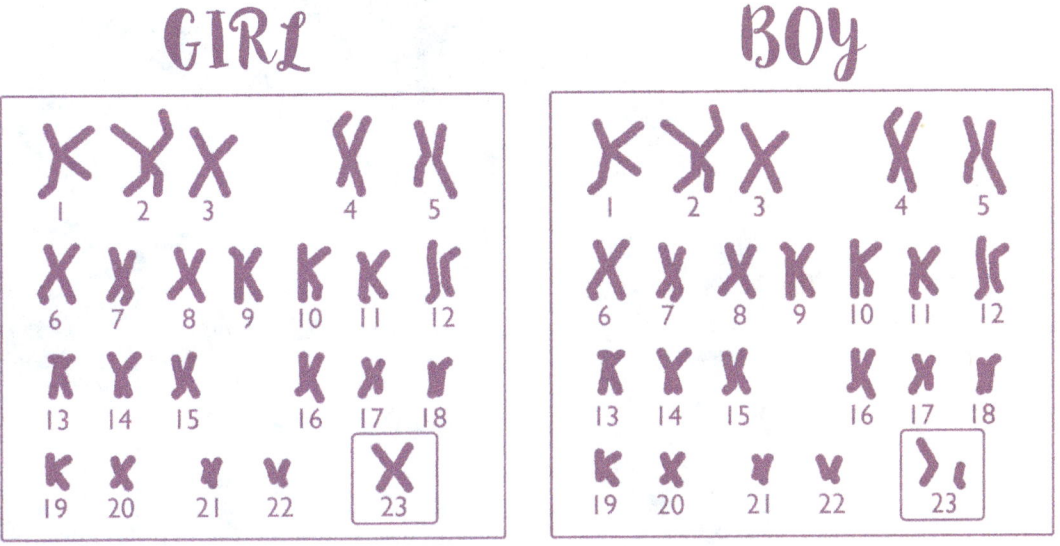

Twenty-two of the pairs are the same in boys and girls.
But the twenty-third pair is different.
In that pair, girls have two x chromosomes while boys have an x and a y.
This never changes.

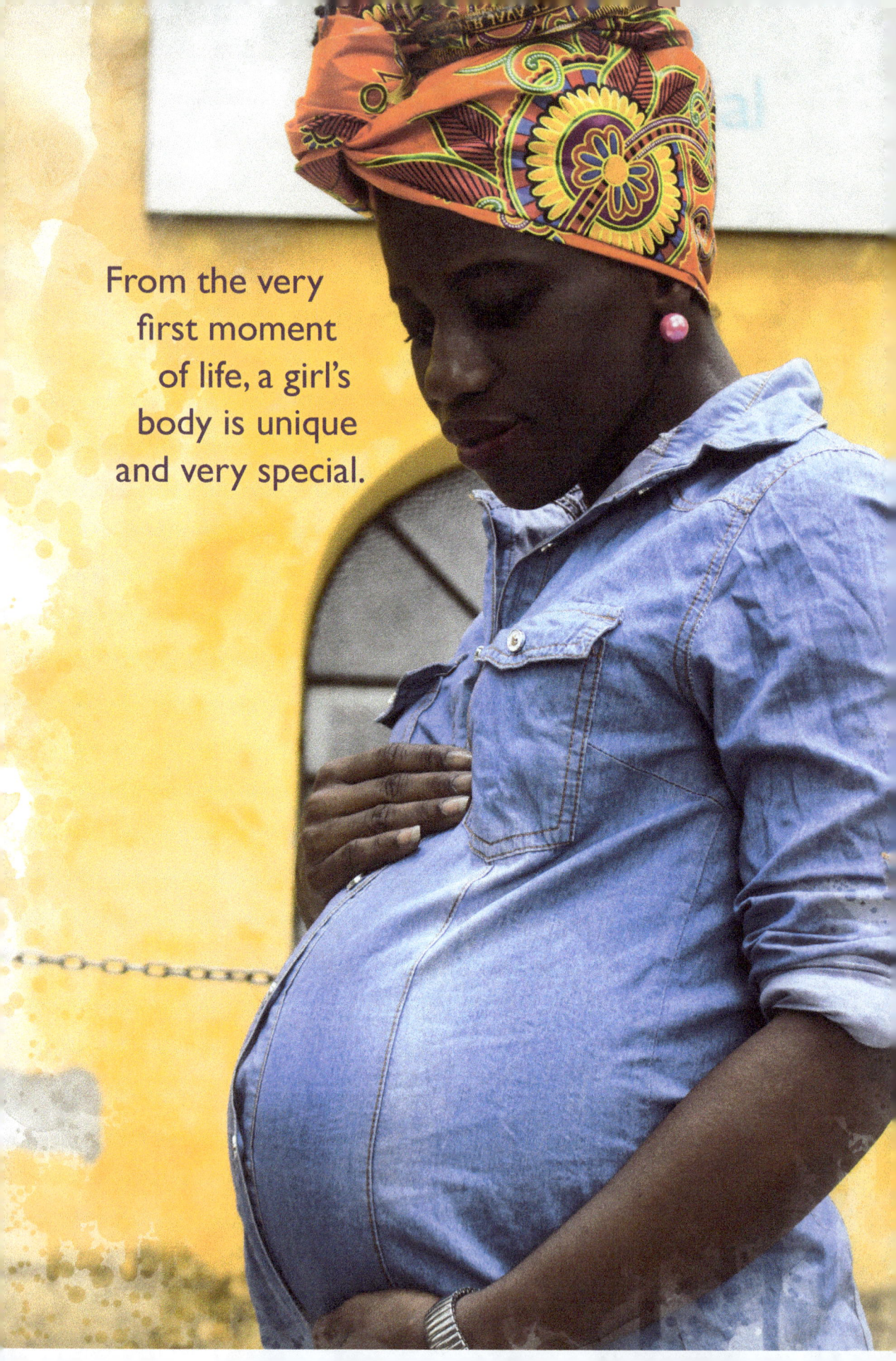

From the very first moment of life, a girl's body is unique and very special.

A big difference between a girl's body
and a boy's is that when she grows up,
she may become a mother and carry a
baby inside her.

Perhaps that's why a lot of little girls
enjoy playing with baby dolls.
To be a mother is a very important job.

But not all girls choose to play with dolls. Some girls love to play soccer.

Some girls enjoy climbing trees,

and some are really good at building projects.

Some girls prefer to paint or make things with their hands.

Some girls love to read books.

Most girls enjoy doing lots of different activities. What is it that you like to do?

Think of some girls you know.
    What do they like to do?
Are they especially good at something?
    Your mother might be a very good cook?

Or perhaps she is a teacher or a doctor?
Do you know a girl who is very kind?

Since the beginning of time, girls have been known for doing many good things.

Florence Nightingale lived in England. She was a nurse who was known for her kindness.

Rosa Parks lived in America. Rosa was very brave and fought against injustice.

Edith Cowan was Australia's first female politician and she used her position to help women and children.

And did you know that men would not have walked on the moon if it were not for a group of African American female mathematicians who helped them get there?

There are lots of true stories of
bold, strong, wise, loving, kind and
brave women.

They may have different
coloured hair or eyes
or skin. They are different
heights and shapes.

But they have something
amazing in common that
never changes – all of
them were once a little girl!

And just like you, these women were
born with abilities and talents
which they used to help others.

Every little girl is created uniquely.
Some are athletic.

Others are musical or enjoy maths or science!

Most little girls look forward to
being a mother one day.

What you do, what you play with,
or what you wear,
does not make you a girl.
It's who you are when you are born.

Your body tells you if you are a boy or a girl.
It's made differently both inside and outside.
And it's very good!

Being a girl is a wonderful thing.
"It's a girl" are some of the loveliest
words any parent could ever hear.
As they look at their little baby,
they might wonder what she will be
like as she grows up.

One thing is for sure — no matter what she does, she will always be a girl, and that is very special.

Message to parents and carers:

Thank you for reading this book to the children in your care. My hope is that through the reading of the simple words, children will be reassured that they are who they are meant to be. They are born in the body that was designed especially for them. And it is good.

Until recently, no one questioned humanity's natural division into female or male. But a strange thing has been happening. This scientific reality is now not only being questioned, but it is being challenged. In a puzzling and retrograde twist, outdated stereotypical interpretations of what it means to be a girl or a boy are being used to channel children into considering, and even exploring, the possibility that they have been 'born in the wrong body'. Kindergartens and schools are introducing books that teach young children that they can choose whether they want to be a girl or a boy. Ideologies are being espoused that maintain there is no such binary entity as a female and a male, but rather that our gender exists on a variable locus. This is an affront to children who naturally have inquisitive minds. The result of this gender-confusing message is an erosion of their right to innocence and wellbeing as they unknowingly participate in a social experiment that can only end badly.

Academics and medical practitioners are warning of an 'epidemic' of confused children presenting to medical clinics, unsure of who they are. Parents are speaking out, describing the incalculable damage being caused to children by gender-fluid teaching in schools and the promotion of the same in the media.

The truth remains that a child's biological sex determines whether they are a girl or a boy. That does not change. The differences between male and female remains one of the miracles of life. No scientist will ever find a way to obliterate the X and Y chromosome and replace it with a G for genderless. No matter what she looks like, no matter what toys she gravitates to, a girl will always be a girl. And this is to be celebrated.

This does not ignore the reality of children born with intersex conditions which, whilst rare, account for a number of genetic or developmental situations. That is a very different conversation. Nor does it discount the suffering of children experiencing gender dysphoria and the need for a compassionate response to relieve that suffering.

But children deserve to be taught the truth in love. That is when they will truly flourish. My prayer is that this book will be used as a tool for meaningful family discussions on what is happening at your daughter's playgroup or school, and within her circle of friends, and that as you read it, you will together marvel at the truly wonderful nature of her female-ness, along with all of the promise that this truth holds.

Wendy Francis

www.ingramcontent.com/pod-product-compliance
Lightning Source LLC
Chambersburg PA
CBHW050640150426
42813CB00054B/1133